ROCK FAS

50 Favorite Quotes

Inspiration for Artists by Famous People

CALI T. ROSSEN

"Unlock Your Heart"   CTR

Rudolfo David *Cover Stylist*
Ernie *Tyler* *Book Cover Photographer*
Andy Haggin & **Cali T. Rossen**
Sunflower Artwork on Fender Electric Guitar
www.rockfashionart.com

A Very Special Thank you to these extraordinary souls I am blessed with in my life:

Chris Rossen: My beloved husband, who loves me unconditionally & consistently cheers me on - especially during those extra challenging days. He is an award winning screenwriter and completed his first novel based on one of his scripts; SYSTEM-UPGRADE. Stay tuned!

Amanda Lee Wasvary: Fashion Designer, Founder & Executive Director of Miss Noho Productions. Amanda's encouragement & guidance led me to take the chance to compete in the Miss North Hollywood Pageant at the El Portal Theater.

Sabrina Chu-Hurd: Peak Models & Talent Agent; who scouted me at the Miss North Hollywood Pageant. She gave me the most amazing support and guidance signing with the Peak Models & Talent Family.

Natasha Duswalt: Author, Model & Founder of Peak Models & Talent Agency and **Craig Duswalt**, Author, Speaker & Founder of Rockstar Marketing Bootcamp for their incredible generosity, encouragement & coaching to create & complete my first book!

A *few more amazing people I love and would like to* acknowledge *for inspiring me:*

Mom & Dad: Pat & Phil Treadwell

Mother & Father in-law: Kate Potter & Dr. Roger Rossen

Family: Deb Van Nort, Brenda Treadwell, Jonathan Treadwell, Justin Bosanquet-Rossen, Heejung Jung, Karen Rood, Lynne & John Feighan, Lalage & Jay Bosanquet and Art & Pixie Powell.

Extended Family: John Lim, Lisa Gold, Andy Haggin, Scott Cohen, Jim Metropole, Rudolfo David, Latha & Venky Kandaswamy, Rick Rosenthal, Mark & Carrie Cohen, Moriah Diamond, Orly Arava, Patricia Prata, Kim Marra, Rachel Bailit, Sonia Maslovskaya, Joycelyne Lew, Michael Blum, Mobin & Gladys Khan, Tammy Cahoon-Guglielmo, Carol Frasier, Michelle Tricca, Kristen Weber, Ed Robles, Perris Alexander, Phoenix Benjamin, Calista Carradine, Dan Scott, Melinda Bonini, Xu & Yuting Sun, Ben & Diana Chen, Rachel Wang and Linda & Ray Tricca.

Gail Marx, Millie Shapiro *Daily Talent*

McKenzie Van Dorne-Rice *Liquid Studios Ent.*

Taylor Boyd, Sarah Stewart & Lacy Serrao *Peak Models*

John Cain, Jeff Dunn, Nina Don and Keith Camacho *Global Touch Partners* and all the Rockstar Master Minders!

ONE

"IMAGINATION IS THE ONLY ESCAPE."

CALI T. ROSSEN

SHOREA ROBUSTA
ARTIST CALI T. ROSSEN

TWO
"UNTIL YOU'RE READY TO LOOK
FOOLISH, YOU'LL NEVER HAVE THE
POSSIBILITY OF BEING GREAT."
CHER

THREE
"CREATIVITY IS CONTAGIOUS
PASS IT ON."
ALBERT EINSTEIN

Cali T. Rossen

LUPINE FIELD
ARTIST CALI T. ROSSEN

6

FOUR
***"LIFE SHRINKS OR EXPANDS IN
PROPORTION TO ONE'S COURAGE."***
ANAIS NIN

FIVE
"AN ARTIST CANNOT FAIL; IT IS A SUCCESS TO BE ONE."
CHARLES HORTON COOLEY

TREE FARM

ARTIST CALI T. ROSSEN

SIX

"IF YOU LET YOUR HEAD GET TOO BIG,
IT'LL BREAK YOUR NECK."

ELVIS PRESLEY

SEVEN
"AGE DOES NOT PROTECT YOU FROM LOVE. BUT LOVE, TO SOME EXTENT, PROTECTS YOU FROM AGE."
ANAIS NIN

Cali T. Rossen

JAMAICAN DAY
ARTIST CHRIS ROSSEN
www.chrisrossen.com

14

EIGHT
"EVERY ARTIST WAS FIRST AN AMATEUR."
RALPH WALDO EMERSON

NINE
"CREATIVITY TAKES COURAGE."
HENRY MATISSE

Cali T. Rossen

ISLANDS
ARTIST CHRIS ROSSEN

TEN
"WE DON'T SEE THINGS AS THEY ARE,
WE SEE THEM AS WE ARE."
ANAIS NIN

Cali T. Rossen

20

ELEVEN
"ART ENABLES US
TO FIND OURSELVES AND LOSE
OURSELVES AT THE SAME TIME."
THOMAS MERTON

HAPPY ANNIVERSARY
ARTIST KATE B. POTTER

TWELVE
***"WE DON'T MAKE MISTAKES,
JUST HAPPY LITTLE ACCIDENTS."***
BOB ROSS

THIRTEEN
"A PICTURE IS A POEM WITHOUT WORDS."
HORACE

GOOD MORNING
ARTIST KATE B. POTTER

FOURTEEN
*"THE PRINCIPLES OF TRUE ART IS NOT
TO PORTRAY, BUT TO EVOKE."*
JERZEY KOSINSKI

FIFTEEN
"*JUST AN OBSERVATION: I'VE NEVER, EVER, EVER, EVER, EVER, HEARD A FEMALE VOICE AS THE NARRATOR OF A MOVIE TRAILER.*"
NEIL DEGRASSE TYSON

C & C
ARTIST MIREU BOSANQUET-ROSSEN

SIXTEEN
"EVERY CHILD IS AN ARTIST. THE PROBLEM IS HOW TO REMAIN AN ARTIST ONCE WE GROW UP."
PABLO PICASSO

SEVENTEEN
"I WANTED TO START A REVOLUTION, USING ART TO BUILD THE SORT OF SOCIETY I MYSELF ENVISIONED."
YAYOI KUSAMA

GUESTS FROM ANOTHER WORLD

ARTIST ANDY HAGGIN

EIGHTEEN
"IN THE MIND OF EVERY ARTIST
THERE IS A MASTERPIECE."
KAI GREENE

NINETEEN
"IF YOU WANT TO RELEASE YOUR
AGGRESSION, GET UP AND DANCE. THAT'S
WHAT ROCK AND ROLL IS ALL ABOUT."
CHUCK BERRY

KOI PANEL
ARTIST MCKENZIE VAN DORNE-RICE
www.mckenzieartstudio.com

TWENTY

*"JUST FIND WHAT WORKS FOR YOU,
WHAT STYLE SUITS YOU BEST, AND JUST
BE CONFIDENT ENOUGH TO ROCK IT."*

ODELL BECKHAM, JR.

Cali T. Rossen

TWENTY ONE
"IF YOU POUR SOME MUSIC ON
WHATEVER'S WRONG,
IT'LL SURE HELP OUT."
LEVON HELM

CHANEL

ARTIST RUDOLFO DAVID

TWENTY TWO
"EVERYTHING IS SCARY IF YOU LOOK AT IT. SO YOU JUST GOT TO LIVE IT."
MARY J. BLIGE

TWENTY THREE
*"LOSE YOUR DREAMS AND
YOU MIGHT LOSE YOUR MIND."*
MICK JAGGER

DAVID BOWIE
ARTIST RUDOLFO DAVID

TWENTY FOUR
"ONE GOOD THING ABOUT MUSIC,
WHEN IT HITS YOU, YOU FEEL NO PAIN."
BOB MARLEY

Cali T. Rossen

TWENTY FIVE
"THE CHIEF ENEMY OF CREATIVITY IS 'GOOD' SENSE."
PABLO PICASSO

Cali T. Rossen

CHIEF
ARTIST DANIEL CLARK

TWENTY SIX
"I THINK THERE IS BEAUTY IN
EVERYTHING. WHAT 'NORMAL' PEOPLE
PERCEIVE AS UGLY, I CAN USUALLY SEE
SOMETHING OF BEAUTY IN IT."
ALEXANDER MCQUEEN

TWENTY SEVEN
"FASHION IS THE ARMOR TO SURVIVE THE REALITY OF EVERYDAY LIFE."
BILL CUNNINGHAM

VIKING

ARTIST DANIEL CLARK

Art Owned by Actor Travis Fimmel

TWENTY EIGHT
"IN DIFFICULT TIMES,
FASHION IS ALWAYS OUTRAGEOUS."
ELSA SCHIAPARELLI

TWENTY NINE
*"THE ESSENCE OF ALL BEAUTIFUL ART,
ALL GREAT ART, IS GRATITUDE."*
FRIEDRICH NIETZSCHE

Cali T. Rossen

GOLDEN TIME
ARTIST CALI ROSSEN

THIRTY
"WE MUST NEVER CONFUSE ELEGANCE
WITH SNOBBERY."
YVES SAINT LAURENT

THIRTY ONE
*"FASHION IS LIKE EATING, YOU
SHOULDN'T STICK TO THE SAME MENU."*
KENZO TAKADA

BLOOM IN
ARTIST CALI T. ROSSEN

THIRTY TWO
"I DON'T DO FASHION. I AM FASHION."
COCO CHANEL

Cali T. Rossen

THIRTY THREE
"THE JOY OF DRESSING IS AN ART."
JOHN GALLIANO

HINKLEY
ARTIST CALI T. ROSSEN

THIRTY FOUR
"MUSIC IS LIKE A PSYCHIATRIST.
YOU CAN TELL YOUR GUITAR THINGS
THAT YOU CAN'T TELL PEOPLE.
AND IT WILL ANSWER YOU WITH THINGS
PEOPLE CAN'T TELL YOU."
PAUL MCCARTNEY

THIRTY FIVE
"I DON'T ALWAYS FEEL FIERCE AND FEARLESS, BUT I DO FEEL LIKE I'M A ROCK STAR AT BEING HUMAN."
TRACEE ELLIS ROSS

JEJU ISLAND
ARTIST CALI T. ROSSEN

THIRTY SIX
"KINDRED SPIRITS,
OUR DEPTHS ARE BOUNDLESS,
THE OCEAN FLOWS WITHIN US."
CALI T. ROSSEN

THIRTY SEVEN
*"IT IS THE FUNCTION OF ART TO
RENEW OUR PERCEPTION. WHAT WE
ARE FAMILIAR WITH WE CEASE TO SEE.
THE WRITER SHAKES UP THE FAMILIAR
SCENE, AND, AS IF BY MAGIC, WE SEE A
NEW MEANING IN IT."*
ANAIS NIN

LOVE
ARTIST CALI T. ROSSEN

THIRTY EIGHT

"CREATIVITY IS ALLOWING YOURSELF TO MAKE MISTAKES. ART IS KNOWING WHICH ONES TO KEEP."

SCOTT ADAMS

Cali T. Rossen

THIRTY NINE
"ART IS STANDING WITH ONE HAND
EXTENDED INTO THE UNIVERSE AND
ONE HAND EXTENDED INTO THE
WORLD, AND LETTING OURSELVES BE A
CONDUIT FOR PASSING ENERGY."
ALBERT EINSTEIN

MAINE
ARTIST CALI T. ROSSEN

FORTY

"YOU HAVE TO SYSTEMATICALLY CREATE CONFUSION, IT SETS CREATIVITY FREE. EVERYTHING THAT IS CONTRADICTORY CREATES LIFE."

SALVADOR DALÍ

FORTY ONE

"I HAVE ALREADY SETTLED IT FOR
MYSELF, SO FLATTERY AND CRITICISM
GO DOWN THE SAME DRAIN
AND I AM QUITE FREE."
GEORGIA O'KEEFFE

RED BERRY BRANCHES
ARTIST CALI T. ROSSEN

FORTY TWO
*"THE WORLD ALWAYS SEEMS BRIGHTER
WHEN YOU'VE JUST MADE SOMETHING
THAT WASN'T THERE BEFORE."*
NEIL GAIMAN

FORTY THREE
"THE COUNTERFEIT INNOVATOR IS
WILDLY SELF-CONFIDENT.
THE REAL ONE IS SCARED TO DEATH."
STEVEN PRESSFIELD

TWINS

PHOTOGRAPHER MICHELLE TRICCA

www.michelletricca.com

FORTY FOUR
**"ART WASN'T SUPPOSED TO LOOK NICE;
IT WAS SUPPOSED TO
MAKE YOU FEEL SOMETHING."**
RAINBOW ROWELL

FORTY FIVE
**"*I HAD SO MUCH FIRE IN ME AND
SO MANY PLANS.*"**
CLAUDE MONET

NANTUCKET
PHOTOGRAPHER MICHELLE TRICCA

FORTY SIX
***"EVERYTHING YOU CAN IMAGINE
IS REAL."***
PABLO PICASSO

FORTY SEVEN
"WORK HARD & PLAY HARD."
T. K. TREADWELL

Cali T. Rossen

ON THE LINE
PHOTOGRAPHER MICHELLE TRICCA

FORTY EIGHT

"ART IS MY LIFE AND MY LIFE IS ART."

YOKO ONO

Cali T. Rossen

FORTY NINE
***"HAVE NO FEAR OF PERFECTION –
YOU'LL NEVER REACH IT."***
SALVADOR DALÍ

Cali T. Rossen

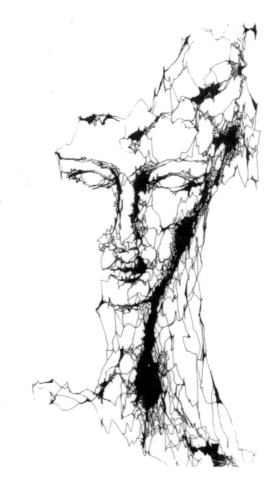

GREECE

ARTIST JAMES METROPOLE

FIFTY
*"GO WITHOUT OR GO WITHIN
AND GO BEYOND."*
CALI T. ROSSEN

BONUS QUOTES
*"HAVING GIFTS THAT DIFFER
ACCORDING TO THE GRACE GIVEN US,
LET US USE THEM."*
ROMANS 12:6

BLUE LADY
ARTIST CALI T. ROSSEN

"MAY ALL BE BLESSED."

DAVID SUMMERSONG

PINK HEART

ARTIST CALI T. ROSSEN

WHALE OF A TAIL
ARTIST CALI T. ROSSEN
(Painting in background)
SCHOODIC POINT
ARTIST CHRIS ROSSEN

BEE HAPPY
ARTIST CALI T. ROSSEN

HARBOR AT LIPARI

ARTIST MCKENZIE VAN DORNE-RICE

PEACE SCULPTURE
ARTIST CALI T. ROSSEN

SPECIAL THANKS!
ARTIST DANIEL CLARK
Pictured alongside his sculptures
Bandon, OR

Cali T. Rossen

SEED OF LIFE SACRED GEOMETRY

Seed of Life - A Universal Symbol. The **Seed of Life** is a symbol for the seven days of creation. The **Seed of Life** is a symbol of blessing and protection passed through generations; it contains the secret of the seven days of the creation.

The Pow Girl Logo is a registered trademark created by coloring in the seed of life with vibrant colors. Our thoughts are like seeds, they sprout into words, then grow into actions, and ultimately become reality.

POW: Power Of Words

THE POW GIRL
PRODUCTIONS
CALI T. ROSSEN
ACTRESS | FILMMAKER | ARTIST

Wikipedia: The Free Encyclopedia. Wikimedia Foundation, Inc. 22 July 2004. Web. 10 Aug. 2004.

Made in the USA
Monee, IL
08 March 2021